The Surname Mason

Susan Morris &
Wendy Bosberry-Scott

The question of surnames, their origins, distribution and history, lies at the heart of genealogy as well as being fascinating in its own right.

In the 1980s and 1990s, long before many genealogical sources were even indexed, let alone online, our Surname Report service provided expert assessments of the origins, history and distribution of selected British surnames, using the sources available at the time.

Now, with so many more sources available, we believe that these reports retain their value as studies of individual surnames, and so we are gradually making the Debrett Surname Archive available online and in print for the first time. Some modern indexes have been consulted to refresh and update the reports.

Debrett Ancestry Research Ltd, PO Box 379,
Winchester SO23 9YQ
Tel: 01962 841904
Email: info@debrettancestry.co.uk
Website: www.debrettancestry.co.uk

CONTENTS

Overview

The use of surnames in England began in the Norman period, when surnames were not necessarily hereditary but usually a form of description. Some described the individual's trade or profession; others were nicknames; some gave the father's Christian name; others gave the individual's place of residence or origin.

Different surnames might be used in different documents, or more than one surname given in one document. Early descriptions were fairly elaborate and by the thirteenth and fourteenth centuries these were simpler, but still variable, and indeed the instability of surnames continued until well into the seventeenth century.

Although some Normans would already have had hereditary surnames on their arrival in Britain, the passing on of a surname from generation to generation only became customary in Britain gradually during the course of the thirteenth and fourteenth centuries. At the end of this period most of the population apparently had surnames.

Variations in the spelling of a family's surname continue to be found until the present century. Before this, as most people could not read or write, the parish clerk or other official would write down the name as they heard it.

There are four main groups of surnames:

A – Local names, which describe a person by his place of residence or origin.

B – Occupational names, which describe a person by his trade or profession.

C – Surnames of relationship, which refer to the Christian name of the father or other important relative.

D – Nicknames or sobriquets, coined to describe a person in terms of his appearance or character.

Many surnames have uncertain origins, but the name Mason (which in this report is treated together with its many variants) clearly falls into Category B.

Origins and early examples

The surname Mason would have originally described a mason, one who worked in stone, and there were of course many of these at the time in which surnames were developing, in the late medieval period. The English word 'mason' was brought to England with the Norman Conquest in two forms: the Old Norman French word was *machun,* but in Central Old French the word was *maçon, mason.* The Norman form, as might be expected, is found most commonly in early literature (from 1205 onwards). Over the centuries the surname has taken on a number of variant forms including Massen, Masson, Machen, Machent, Machin, Machon and several of these reflect this early Norman form.

The earliest example of the surname that has been found was John Macun who is mentioned in a charter from London dated ca 1130 (cited in Reaney & Wilson, *English Surnames,* 1995). At this date the name is unlikely to have been hereditary so we can tentatively assume that John was himself a mason.

Other early examples of the surname cited by Reaney and Wilson are as follows:

1193	Ace le mazun	Herefordshire Pipe Rolls
12c	Richard machun	Lincolnshire
1200	Roger le Mason	Oxfordshire: Cartulary of Oseney Abbey
1203	Godfrey le Mascun	Essex Feet of Fines
1279	Osbert le Masson	Oxfordshire Hundred Rolls

1279	Adam le Machon	Northumberland Assizes
1284	Richard Machen	Staffordshire Assizes
1439	Thomas Machyn	Warwickshire deeds

It can be seen that in the thirteenth century the surname was widespread in England and was found a variety of different forms.

In 1892 W J Hardy and W Page published *A Calendar to the Feet of Fines for London and Middlesex 1189-1485*, in which there are two Mason references, one to le Masoun and another to le Mazon, shown below. (The fine was a means of conveying or settling freehold property, from the reign of Richard I up to 1834, when a Statute was passed to abolish the method and set up a simpler way of achieving matters.)

> John son of Ralph le Masoun and Michael le Sergant and Gervase Parmentar. One messuage and eight acres of land in Holeborne, Purtepol and Bradeford. These are acknowledged to be the right of the said John, who in exchange, give to Michael and Gervase a moiety of the croft which Gamel held and half an acre of land this side of (*citra*) Purtepol, towards the south. 8 John [1206/7]

> Henry le Mazon by Peter de Hamme and Robert de Dunwich and Alice his wife. One messuage in the parish of St Andrew 'de Holeburn' without the Bar London. I Edward I [1272/3]

M A Lower's *Patronymica Brittanica* (1860), a pioneering and still useful British surname dictionary, gives the following explanation for the surname:

4

Mason
1. The occupation. Le Mason, Le Masson, Le Masun –
Rotuli Hundredorum
2. A township in Northumberland.

This led us to consult Eilert Ekwall's *Oxford Dictionary of English Place Names* (1987), which draws upon a general survey of early and secondary sources including charters, deeds, the Domesday Book and maps, to chart the various early forms of a given place name and thus explain its meaning. Ekwall includes Mason in his dictionary:

> **Mason** Northumberland – *Mærheard's fen*
> Merdisfen   1242 The Book of Fees
> Merdefen   1242 Close Rolls
> Merdesfen   1260-3 Newcastle Deeds

Thus the surname derives from an occupation whereas the place name takes its origins from the personal name *Mærheard*. None of the early forms found suggest a place name origin, and it would seem that the form Mason is a relatively modern development of the place name, so on the whole it is unlikely that instances of the surname Mason derive from the place name, although it would be necessary to trace back an individual family into the middle ages to prove this.

It should be added that, in the case of the surname Machin, the older surname authorities such as Bardsley and Henry Harrison (*Surnames of the United Kingdom*, 2 vols, London, 1918) had a different theory of the origins of the name, suggesting that it derived from the Biblical name Matthew and is an Anglicisation of the Hebrew name which means 'Gift of Jehovah'. Bardsley specifically states that Machin means 'Baptised the son of Matthew' and was also found as an Old French nickname for Matthew (Mace, Mache, Machon, Machin). He adds that the surname was particularly common in Yorkshire: 'it has left an indelible mark upon Yorkshire nomenclature', but it was found in every district of England. This theory has been rejected by modern surname scholars.

Distribution

Two volumes of the *English Surnames Series* (which is very incomplete) include discussions of the surname Mason:

Yorkshire: West Riding (Vol I)

Mason shown as an occupational name that became a surname.

Example given: John Mason, a mason in Ripon in 1379.

In the York Subsidy Roll for 1524, there were 8 taxpayers named Mason out of 864, in 1965 there were 81.

Norfolk & Suffolk Surnames in the Middle Ages (Vol II)

Margery le Mazoun, of Terrington, Norfolk in 1329/30, is cited as an early example of an hereditary surname, as a woman would not normally be given an occupational name. The name Mason was widely scattered in East Anglia in the fourteenth century, and not confined to large towns or any one district where their trade would be expected. One Johannes le Macon, a mason in Staverton, Suffolk was noted as a serf in 1200. Joel le Mascun, a free peasant holding a half ferling in Nutcot was party to a fine in 1249 and Joel le Mazon was suitor to Crown Please in 1238.

H R Moulton's *Palaeography, Genealogy and Topography* is primarily a sale catalogue printed in the 1930s listing historical documents, ancient charters, leases, court rolls *etc.*, and is useful as a national overview of surname distribution. Here there were, as expected, many entries for the name Mason *etc*.

Essex

22 July 1614

Deed of Limitations of Uses by the Rt Hon Jane Lady Berkeley for the manors of Wyvenhoe, Bentley and Battleswick *etc*. Witnesses: Mich Stanhope, William Sincklay, Richard Mason, Richard Marske, Thomas Wells. Signature of Jane Berkley. Fragment of seal. 30/-

22 May 1731

Marriage settlement. Byran Reeve Knowlys of Manningtree co Essex of 1st part, Michael Hills of Colchester, Thomas Mason of Manningtree of 2nd part Elizabeth Hills daughter of said Michael of 3rd part on marriage o Bryan Reeve to Elizabeth Hills. Witnesses: James Vanderzee, Robert Price. Signatures of all parties. 30/-

Hampshire

7 September 1563

Bargain and Sale. Hartley Wintney. Sir John Masone Knt to John Abbott of Hartley Wintney co Southampton. 21/-

24 November 1607

Letters patent of James I under the great seal granting a licence to John Mason, esquire, and Frances his wife to alienate to Edward lord Zouche and William Randoll gent and the heirs of the said Edward one messuage *etc* in Wintney co Southampton. Westminster 24 November 5 James I. Faded and rubbed. £1/1/-

1 April 1618

Assignment. Hartley Wintney manor. Sir Thomas
Penruddock of Hale county Southampton knt.
Laurence Rudyard Frances Mason sister to Sir
Thomas and wife of John Mason. To Edward Topsell
and Richard Cooke of London. Witnesses: George
Perry, Thomas Byrd, Thomas Butler and others.
Signatures of parties of 1st part. 3 Armorial seals. 30/-

Kent

12 February 1720

Exemplification under the seal of the common Pleas
of a recovery suffered in Hilary Term 6 George I
between Shadra Blundell esq, demandant and George
Fuller gent tenant concerning messuages and land in
East Greenwich co Kent. Vouchees: Christopher
Mason esq, Garrett Edmonds. 30/-

Lincolnshire

4 October 1471

Grant. Holton cum Beckering. John Langlay of
Wickenby co Lincoln to James West of Holton cum
Berkering co Lincoln Thomas Blaw of Holton cum
Beckering co Lincoln John Mason of Holton cum
Beckering co Lincoln. £2

16 July 1731

Release on marriage agreement. Henry Money of
Deeping St James co Linc to William Holmes of
Deeping St James co Linc to marriage of William
Holmes to Ann daughter of said Henry. Witnesses:
John Hickling, Thomas Mason. Mark of Henry
Money. 1 seal. 30/-

London & Middlesex

10 January 1739

Indenture of bargain and sale by Sarles Goatley of Cobree in Boxley co Kent esq to Anne French of Maidstone co Kent spinster of messuages in Hoxton in St Leonard Shoreditch co Middx with a garden adjoining the said messuages with the proviso that if Sarles Goatley pay Anne French £512 10s 0d on 10th July next ensuing then this deed shall be void. Witnesses: Thomas Atkins, John Mason. Signature Sarles Goatley. 1 seal. 25/-

Northamptonshire

27 September 1598

Indenture of bargain and sale by William Masonne of Creke or Creicke co Northampton husbandman to William Watts of Creke or Cricke husbandman and Richard his son of lands in Creke or Cricke. Witnesses: John Bucknell, Hugon Paule, Richard Masonne, marke of Richard Greene, William Mabie, John Sabinne, Robert Shatswell. Signature: Will [Masonne]. 20/-

Staffordshire

11 November 1314

Demise by Sarah, daughter of Ivo le Botiler of Eliston, to Ivo her father. Witnesses: Peter le Botiler, Robert de Reynes, John le Lord, Robert de Thorney, William Bertram, Simon le Taylour, Stephen le Masoun. Seal. £3/3/-

Surrey

15 September 1512

Quitclaim by Thomas Hayward of Walton co Surrey 'yoman' to John Grover of Kyngeston upon Thames in the same county of all his right in lands in the parish of Wokkyng called Benryth, Chamberlondes, Claylake londes, 33a[cres] of land, 3a[cres] of pasture formerly of John Castell and Isabel his wife and a messuages, garden and 10 a[cres] of land called Spynners in Wokkyng. Dated at Wokkyng 15 September 4 Henry VIII. Portion of seal. [endorsed] Witnesses: Thomas Cheverell, Robert Hayward, John Jobson, Thomas Jescelyn, William Barwyk, Robert Barton, John Smyth, Richard Gaddesdon, John Lane, Richard Davy, Thomas Wysdom, William Machyn and many others. 30/-

Sussex
26 December 1370
Grant by Thomas Bokyngham the elder of New Shorham to William Pratun tailor of lands in Old Shorham viz: 1 acre in the Midmestefordlangg of the Hamme between the land of the abbot of Battle and the land late of John de Abberbury, ½ acre in the Southmesterforlangg of the Hamme between the land of Richard Fraunk and the land of John de Abberbury, ½ acre by Westetheweye between the land of John de Abberbury and the land of Richard Fraunk, ½ acre ½ rood upon Wreycountlithe between Littedoune and the land of William Kyllard, ½ acre in Bereforlangg on the Ystleyne between the land of John Alayn and the land of John de Abberbury, ½ rood in Sharforlangg at the head of the said ½ acre between the land of William Ysthenfelde and the land of John de Abberbury, 1 rood in the Southmestershotes between the land of William Kyllard and the land of John de Abberbury, ½ acre in the Northmesterforangg on the Ystleyne between the land of John Masson and the land of John Bernard. Witnesses: John atte Hyde, William Avenel, Richard Fraunk, Roger Ronge, Ralph Yder, John Griffyn, Edmund Proo, Old Shorham. 26 December 44 Edward III. Fragment of seal. £3/10/-

Yorkshire
1 August 1615
Bargain and sale. Monkhill in Pontefract. Philipp
Darell of London to Thomas Cattall of Pontefract.
Witnesses: Thomas Sanwith, Henry Mason.
Signature: Phi Darell. 21/-

Again this shows how the name was fairly widespread
across the country.

In 1890 H B Guppy published his *Homes of Family
Names in Great Britain*, still the only published work on
surname distribution in Britain as a whole. His work
was based on printed genealogies and a survey of
county directories for the 1880s, in which he looked
especially at the names of farmers, reasoning that they
were among the most stable groups in society. Guppy
restricted his study to names which appeared in a
proportion of 7:10,000 or higher. As can be seen from the
list below, the name was fairly widely represented
throughout England as Mason, with a noticeable
concentration of the variant Machin in the centre of
England.

Machin
Derbyshire – 9
Gloucestershire – 8
Lincolnshire – 10
Nottinghamshire – 32
Staffordshire – 12

Mason
Cambridgeshire – 60
Cheshire – 30
Derbyshire – 20
Devon – 8

Essex – 21
Herefordshire   – 17
Huntingdonshire – 10
Lancashire - 30
Leicestershire & Rutland – 21
Lincolnshire – 22
Norfolk – 15
Northamptonshire – 20
Shropshire – 22
Staffordshire – 20
Suffolk – 11
Surrey – 11
Warwickshire   – 18
Worcestershire – 14
Yorkshire west – 25
Yorkshire north & east – 23

Guppy also noted that Machin was a well-known Gloucestershire name in the sixteenth century, through to the eighteenth century, when a gentry family of that name was found in Bicknor English and Acton. Machins was a name he found in Nottinghamshire, although not in sufficient numbers to appear in the main body of his work, with small showings of this variant in other midland counties. A Machins was found in the Freeholders List in Nottinghamshire in 1698.

Guppy observed that Mason had a very poor showing in the southern coastal counties and was entirely absent in some; this was also true of the counties north of Lancashire and Yorkshire. He found Mason most strongly represented in Cambridgeshire, followed by Cheshire, Lancashire and Yorkshire. The variant Machon was found in Lincolnshire.

George F Black, in *The Surnames of Scotland* (1946), states that 'there is no evidence that, in Scotland, this surname had any other origin than from the occupation. In the Middle Ages we found it Latinised *cementarius...*'. Black's work also lists examples of the surname found in various Scottish deeds and records:

C1180 Magister Roger cementarius de Forfar witnessed a charter by Ingelram de Balliol.

1271 Richard the Mason was burgess of Aberdeen

1288 John le Massun or Le Macune of Gascony had a claim against the bishop of St Andrews

1307 William dictus Masceon who had a charter of land in the burgh of Berwick in [that year] is probably William Maceoun de Berwick who received a payment from Exchequer in 1327

1317 William dictus Maceon was burgess of Peebles

1360 Nicholas cementarius cusumar of Stirling appears in the following year as Nicholas Masoun

1388 Thomas Mason or Masson a kinsman of Robert earl of Fife claimed the office of prior of Loch Leven

1436 Peter Masoune was canon of Dunkeld

1463 David Mayssone was a prebyter of Glasgow

16C Prominent Mason family in Orkney also shown as Meason, Maison and Massoun.

18-19C Francis Masson pioneer of botanical science in South Africa was born in Aberdeen in 1741, died 1805

The name Mason is not included in Edward MacLysaght's *Guide to Irish Surnames* (1965) but in T J and Prys Morgan's *Welsh Surnames* (1985) we found a reference to Machen which is a village in south west Gwent.

Many of the sources available for charting surname distribution through the centuries are necessarily confined to the wealthier sectors of the population: in general, nobody wanted to know the names of the poor but the names of those with money or land were naturally of interest to the authorities. However, one source that covers the whole of the social spectrum is provided by English parish registers, the earliest of which began in 1538 following a mandate that all parish priests should keep a weekly record of all baptisms, marriages and burials that took place in their parish. A survey of a cross section of parish registers for the years 1601 and 1602 was carried out in 1910 by F K and S Hitching; incidences of a particular surname are noted by parish and county, although with no indication of numbers of references.

1601
Buckinghamshire: Great Hampden – Mason
Cambridgeshire: Lolworth – Mason
Cumberland: Dalston   – Mayson
Gloucestershire: Cheltenham   – Mason
Lancashire: Brindle – Mason
Lancashire: Bury – Maconde
Lancashire: Cockerham – Mason
Lancashire: Croston – Machon
Lancashire: Eccles – Mason
Lancashire: Ormskirk – Mason
Lancashire: Wigan – Mason
Leicestershire: Scraptoft – Mason
London: St Vedast Foster Lane – Masson
London: French Church Threadneedle Street – Macon
Middlesex: Greenford – Mason
Norfolk: Heacham – Mason
Northumberland: Berwick upon Tweed – Mason
Staffordshire: Walsall St Matthew – Mason

Suffolk: Ingham – Mason
Surrey: Bermondsey – Mason
Yorkshire: Ecclesfield   – Mason
Yorkshire: Leeds – Mayson
Yorkshire: Roos All Saints – Mason
Yorkshire: Stokesley – Masons
Yorkshire: Terrington   – Mason
Yorkshire: York Minster, All Saints – Mason

Again, the most common variant of the name was Mason, but other examples such as Mayson appeared in Cumberland, Lancashire and Yorkshire, and Mac(h)on in London and Lancashire.   In 1602 Mayson appeared in County Durham but still had a showing in Yorkshire; again the most widely used variant found was Mason.

1602
County Durham: Durham St Oswald – Mayson
Dorset: Powerstock & West Milton – Mason
Gloucestershire: Charlton King's – Machin
Gloucestershire: Cheltenham – Mason
Hampshire: Burghclere – Mason
Lancashire: Ormskirk – Mason
Lancashire: Chipping – Mason
Lancashire: Cockerham – Mason
Lancashire: Lancaster – Masone
Lancashire: Manchester Cathedral – Mason
London: French Church Threedneedle Street – Macon
London: St Mary Aldermary – Mason
Middlesex: Clerkenwell St James – Mason
Norfolk: Old Buckenham – Mason
Nottinghamshire: Kneeton – Masone
Shropshire: Broomfield – Masonne
Shropshire: Donington – Mason
Shropshire: Wem – Mason
Shropshire: Clunbury – Mason
Shropshire: Lydham – Mason

Suffolk: Little Saxham – Mason
Suffolk: Ingham – Mason
Yorkshire: Dewsbury   – Masonn
Yorkshire: Leeds St Peter – Mayson
Yorkshire: Roos All Saints – Mason

A useful guide to the distribution of surnames for the sixteenth, seventeenth and eighteenth centuries in England is provided by the indexes to wills proved, and administrations granted, at the Prerogative Court of (the Archbishop of) Canterbury, in London, which had superior jurisdiction over local ecclesiastical courts where wills were proved until 1858. The PCC thus provides a national index, although it is not a completely representative one, as testators whose wills were proved in the PCC were mostly among the wealthier members of society, and a disproportionate number of them were from London or Middlesex.

A search of the printed indexes for the years 1558 to 1583; 1584 to 1604; 1605 to 1619; 1620 to 1629; 1653 to 1656; 1657 to 1660; 1661 to 1670; 1671 to 1675; 1676 to 1685; 1686 to 1693; 1694 to 1700; 1701 to 1749; and 1750 to 1800 found the following entries for Mason with other variants appearing in very small numbers:

1558-1599
Buckinghamshire: Mason (1)
Dorset: Mason (2); also noted Macham
Essex: Mason (1)
Gloucestershire: Mason (1); also noted Machin
Hampshire: Mason (1)
Herefordshire: Mason (2); also noted Machine
Kent: Mason (1)
Lancashire: only found Machon
Lincolnshire: Mason (1)

17

London & Middlesex: Mason (11); also noted Macham
and Machin
Monmouthshire: Mason (2)
Norfolk: Mason (4)
Shropshire: Mason (2); also noted Machin
Somerset: only found Macham
Suffolk: Mason (3)
Surrey: only found Machon
Wiltshire: Mason (3)
Worcestershire: Mason (1)

The variant Mayson was not found in the indexes at this period, indicating that this form might have been specifically found in northern counties such as Lancashire and Yorkshire, since these counties are not well represented in the PCC indexes.

Seventeenth Century
Berkshire: Mason (5)
Cambridgeshire: Mason (3)
Cheshire: Mason (1)
Cork: Mason (1)
Cornwall: Mason (1)
Cumberland: Mason (1)
Denbighshire: Mason (1)
Derbyshire: Mason (4)
Devon: Mason (3)
Dorset: Mason (3)
Durham: Mason (1); also noted Machon
Essex: Mason (6); also noted Makin(s)
Glamorganshire: Mason (1)
Gloucestershire: Mason (15); also noted Machen and
Machin
Hampshire: Mason (8); also noted Masson
Herefordshire: Mason (6); also noted Machin
Hertfordshire: Mason (1)
Huntingdonshire: Mason (6)

In partibus transmarinus: Mason (10); also noted
   Machin
Kent: Mason (12); also noted Machin and Macune
Lancashire: Mason (3)
Leicestershire: Mason (2)
Lincolnshire: Mason (6)
London & Middlesex: Mason (65); also noted Machin,
Le Machon, Masson and Massome
Monmouthshire: Mason (2)
Norfolk: Mason (9); also noted Machin and Makyns
Northamptonshire: Mason (3)
Nottinghamshire: Mason (2); also noted Machin
Oxfordshire: Mason (4); also noted Masson, Machin
   and Machen
Orkney: Mason (1)
Radnor: Mason (1)
Rutland: Mason (1)
Shropshire: Mason (7)
Somerset: Mason (3); also noted Massan
Staffordshire: Mason (5); also noted Machin
Suffolk: Mason (12); also noted Masson
Surrey: Mason (15)
Sussex: Mason (1); also noted Machin
Wales: Mason (1)
Warwickshire: Mason (8)
Wiltshire: Mason (3)
Worcestershire: Mason (5); also noted Machin and
   Masons
Yorkshire: Mason (8); also noted Mayson

Mayson appears in Yorkshire and other variants were
found such as Makyns and possibly Massome and
Massan.

Eighteenth Century
Bedfordshire: Mason (2)
Berkshire: Mason (11); also noted Machin and
   Machen

19

Buckinghamshire: Mason (18)

Cambridgeshire: Mason (6)

Cornwall: Mason (3)

Devon: Mason (3)

Durham: Mason (2)

Essex: Mason (21)

Gloucestershire: Mason (17); also noted Machon, Machen, Machin and Mayson

Hampshire: Mason (9)

Herefordshire: Mason (6); also noted Machen

Hertfordshire: Mason (12); also noted Machin

Huntingdonshire: Mason (4)

In partibus transmarinus (overseas) Mason (135); also noted Masson, Machon, Masoner, Mayson and Machin

Ireland: Mason (1); also noted Machon

Jersey: only found Machon

Kent: Mason (37); also noted Machin, Masson and Machen

Lancashire: Mason (1)

Leicestershire: Mason (3)

Lincolnshire: Mason (3); also noted Masson

London & Middlesex: Mason (233); also noted Machan, Machen, Maichen, Machin, Masson, Machon and Mayson

Monmouthshire: Mason (6)

Montgomeryshire: Mason (1)

Norfolk: Mason (9)

Northamptonshire: Mason (7)

Nottinghamshire: Mason (3); also noted Machin

Oxfordshire: Mason (12)

Pembrokeshire: Mason (2)

Rutland: Mason (1)

Scotland: Mason (1)

Shropshire: Mason (7); also noted Machin

Somerset: Mason (1); also noted Mayson

Staffordshire: Mason (7)

Suffolk: Mason (3); also noted Machin

Surrey: Mason (51)
Sussex: Mason (4)
Warwickshire: Mason (12); also noted Machin
Wiltshire: Mason (1)
Worcestershire: Mason (4); also noted Machin
Yorkshire: Mason (1)

After London and Middlesex, the greatest showing of the name in the PCC indexes for the eighteenth century, rather unusually, was for overseas testators. Many of these would have been servicemen.

For the nineteenth century, H B Guppy's survey has been mentioned above. Another important Victorian source is the *Return of Owners of Land* of 1873, sometimes known as the Modern Domesday Book. This source lists, county by county, every owner of an acre of land or more, with their residence (not necessarily the address of their property) and the acreage of their holding.

Return of Owners of Land
Anglesey – Mason (2)
Bedfordshire – Mason (1)
Berkshire – Mason (1)
Buckinghamshire – Mason (11)
Cambridgeshire – Mason (30)
Cardiganshire – Mason (5)
Cheshire – Machin (3); Makin (1); Mason (7)
Cornwall – Mason (7)
Denbighshire – Mason (2)
Derbyshire – Machin (8); Mason (9)
Devon – Mason (5)
Dorset – Mason (1)
Durham – Mason (3)
Essex – Mason (16)
Gloucestershire – Masen (1); Mason (9)
Hampshire – Mason (6)

Herefordshire – Mason (24)
Hertfordshire – Mason (7)
Huntingdon – Mason (8)
Kent – Masen (1); Mason (4)
Lancashire – Makin (5); Mason (29); Mayson (2)
Leicestershire – Mason (10)
Lincolnshire – Machin (6); Machon (1); Mason (47)
Middlesex – Mason (7)
Monmouthshire – Machen (1); Mason (1)
Norfolk – Mason (15)
Northamptonshire – Mason (3)
Northumberland – Mason (6)
Nottinghamshire – Machin (6); Mason (10)
Oxfordshire – Makins (1); Mason (3)
Radnorshire – Mason (1)
Rutland – Mason (1)
Shropshire – Mason (5)
Somerset – Mason (3)
Staffordshire – Machin (2); Mason (9)
Suffolk – Makens (1); Makin (2); Making (1);
   Makins (1); Mason (6)
Surrey – Mason (11)
Sussex – Mason (2)
Warwickshire – Machin (1); Mason (11)
Westmoreland – Mason (7)
Wiltshire – Mason (2)
Worcestershire – Mason (6)
Yorkshire East – Machon (1); Masin (1); Mason (1)
Yorkshire North – Mason (17)
Yorkshire West – Machen (2); Machin (4); Makin (5);
   Makins (1); Mason (28)

Most entries were for Mason but other variants such as Machin, Makin *etc* were found fairly widely spread across the country.

In *The Personal Names of the Isle of Man* (1937) J J Kneen notes the use of the variant Mazon on the island, with examples from 1609 and 1703:

> **Mason** Mason (1511), Masson (1655), Mazon (1703)
> A mason. 'Every Mazon, Carpenter, Shipwright, Hooper, Slater, Thatcher, thatching after the English fashion, and Joiner, shall have the Day, with Meat and Drink, iiijd. And not above, being sufficient Workmen.' Manx Statutes AD 1609.

The first decennial census return in England, Scotland and Wales was taken in 1801, but personal information was only recorded from 1841 onwards. From 1851, the age, occupation and birthplace is given for each member of the household, and so these records provide invaluable genealogical information as well as a fascinating 'snapshot' of the family in the nineteenth century. The latest return currently open to public inspection is that of 1911 and there are now national indexes to the returns from 1841 onwards, although these indexes are not wholly reliable. Using these indexes, we found the following numbers for Mason, Massen, Masson, Machon, Machent, Machin, Machon and Mazon, in England, Scotland and Wales:

6 June 1841
Mason (24,467)
Massen (21)
Masson (1197)
Machon (372)
Machent (10)
Machin (1697)
Machon (372)

30 March 1851
Mason (26,457)
Massen (42)
Masson (1281)
Machon (377)
Machent (7)
Machin (1881)
Machon (377)
Mazon (29)

7 April 1861
Mason (28,398)
Massen (42)
Masson (1672)
Machon (281)
Machent (9)
Machin (1900)
Machon (281)
Mazon (10)

2 April 1871
Mason (34,543)
Massen (27)
Masson (1542)
Machon (354)
Machent (12)
Machin (2661)
Machon (354)
Mazon (1)

3 April 1881
Mason (40,202)
Massen (58)
Masson (1792)
Machon (373)
Machent (42)
Machin (3001)
Machon (373)

Mazon (1)

5 April 1891
Mason (43,310)
Massen (51)
Masson (2080)
Machon (377)
Machent (32)
Machin (3137)
Machon (377)
Mazon (21)

31 March 1901
Mason (50,065)
Massen (72)
Masson (2248)
Machon (425)
Machent (46)
Machin (3988)
Machon (425)
Mazon (2)

2 April 1911
Mason (52,413)
Massen (101)
Masson (531)
Machon (415)
Machent (60)
Machin (4262)
Machon (415)
Mazon (2)

As expected, the greatest numbers were found for Mason, with Machin, the second largest group, showing barely ten per cent of the numbers of Mason. The variant Mazon, which as we have seen was known in the Isle of Man from at least the early seventeenth century, was found in 1851 in Wales, with two examples in England. By 1861, Mazon had spread to England. In 1881 the only Mazon found in the indexes was for a William J Mazon, who was serving in the Royal Navy. The indexes for 1891 show 21 Mazon entries, mainly in Wales, and this suggests that the 1871 and 1881 indexes may be faulty or that families of the name Mazon were recorded under Mason or another variant.

Famous bearers of the name & Coats of Arms

There are many entries in the first edition of *The Dictionary of National Biography* for the British Isles for the name Mason. Most are clerics and authors; some of the other Mason entries were as follows:

> Charles Mason (1730-1787) – astronomer
> Francis Mason (1837-1886) – surgeon
> George Heming Mason (1818-1872) – painter
> James Mason (fl 1743-1783 – landscape engraver
> Sir John Mason (1503-1566) – statesman
> John Mason (1586-1635) – founder of New Hampshire
> Sir Josiah Mason (1796-1881) – pen manufacturer and
>   philanthropist
> Martin Mason (fl 1650-1676) – Quaker
> William Monck Mason (1775-1859) – historian

Another famous Mason is Nicholas Berkeley Mason, born 1944, better known as Nick Mason, the drummer for Pink Floyd and collector of classic cars. His father, Bill Mason, was a documentary film maker.

There were also entries for men named Machen, Machin, Machon and Masson:

> Thomas Machen (1568-1614) – fellow of Magdalen
>   College, Oxford
> Henry Machin or Machyn (?1498-?1563) – diarist
> John Machin (1624-1664) – ejected non-conformist
> John Machin (d1751) – astronomer
> Lewis Machin (fl 1608) – author
> Robert Machin or Macham (fl 1344) – legendary
>   discover of Madeira

John Machon (1572-?1640) – cleric
David Masson (1822-1907) – biographer and editor
Sir David Orme Masson (1858-1937) – chemist
Francis Masson (1741-1805) – gardener and botanist
George Joseph Gustave Masson (1819-1888) –
  educational writer

There are 20 coats of arms listed in Burke's *General Armory* granted to men of the name Mason (and two for the Mason's Company of London and Edinburgh), and a further grant of arms for Mason is described in *General Armory II* by C Humphrey-Smith (1972), who also notes amendments to Burke and shows the arms for the Masons' company of Newcastle upon Tyne. We noted the following coats of arms for Machen, Machin and Machon:

Machen (Eastbach Court and Whitemead park co Gloucester; descended from Thomas Machin, three times Mayor of Gloucester, buried in that city in 2614; granted to Richard Machen co Gloucester 1615; the present representative is Rev Edward Machen of Eastbach Court and Whitemead Park [1884]) Gules a fesse vair between three pelicans' heads erased or, vulning themselves proper. Crest – A pelican's head erased or.

Machen, Machin or Machon - same arms as Machen of Eastbach court. Crest – A lion's head erased sable on the head a cap of Maintenance or.

Machon (Machon Bank near Sheffield; removed to Durham). Gules a fess vair between three swans' heads erased argent and a canton of the last.

Machon (Sherburn House, Durham) – same arms.

28

Machon – (co York) Gules a fess vair between three pelican's heads argent vulning themselves proper a canton argent.

Printed Genealogies

There are numerous printed genealogies of Mason families and we also include here genealogies of families named Machen, Machin and Machon:

Machen/Machin/Machon
Miscellanea Genealogica et Heraldica 4th series, v, 195
Bristol & Gloucestershire Archaeological Society, lxiv, 96
Burke's *Landed Gentry* 1846-52, 1858, 1863, 1871, 1879, 1886, 1894, 1937, 1952, 1972
W D Sweeting, *A Record of the Family of Debenham of Suffolk* (1909) 9
Joseph Hunter, *Hallamshire: The History and Topography of the parish of Sheffield* (London 1819) 372
Robert Surtees, *The History and Antiquities of the County Palatine of Durham* (London 1816-40) i, 143
Foster, *Visitations of Durham* 219
Harleian Society xxi, 106

Mason
Burke's *Peerage and Baronetage* 1970
Burke's *Landed Gentry* 1846-52, 1858, 1863, 1871, 1882, 1886, 1894, 1937, 1952
Burke's *Distinguished Families of the USA*
Burke's *Commoners* iv, 354
The East Anglian Pedigrees
Harleian Society xci, 150; viii, 132; xvii, 85-87; xxix, 353; xxxvii, 201; xxxviii, 792; xlii, 191
Miscellanea Genealogica & Heraldica 5th series, vi, 67
The Pedigree Register (1907-16) ii, 132
F A Crisp, *Visitations of England & Wales* xv, 132
Notes & Queries xii, 31; 4th series, xii, 87, 335, 418
Ruvigny, *The Anne of Exeter Volume* (Essex) (1907) 97

Ruvigny, *The Mortimer Percy Volume part I* (1911) 145, 257

Transactions of the Shropshire Archaeological Society xlvi, 177

J E Griffith, *Pedigrees of Anglesey & Carnarvonshire Families* (1914) 81

B Thistlethwaite, *The Thistlethwaite Family: A Study in Genealogy* (1910) i 41

R M Howard, *Records and Letters of the Family of the Longs of Longville, Jamaica and Hampton Lodge, Surrey* (1925) i, 213

T A Emmet, *The Emmet Family* (NY 1898) 361

W Rye, *Norfolk Families* (1915) 538, 539

J G White, *Historical and Topographical Notes etc on Buttevant* (1905-16, Cork Historical Society) iii, 110

Lewys Dwnn, *Heraldic Visitations of Wales and part of the Marches 1586 & 1613* (Llandovery 1846) ii, 165

William Berry, *Pedigrees of the Families of Kent* (London 1830) 328, 336

Bibliotheca Topographica Britannica vii Parts i & ii 351

Foster, *Yorkshire Pedigrees*

John Nichols, *The History and Antiquities of the County of Leicester* (London 1795-1807) iii, 1148

Surtees Society liv, 218

Archdall, *Lodge's Peerage* iii, 177

Carthew, *West and East Bradenham* 159

Hasted *Kent* 81

New England Register xv 117, 217, 318; xvii 39, 214; xviii, 245

William Cudworth, *Histories of Bolton and Bowling* 218

H E Smith, *Annals of Smith of Balby* 217

Summary

To conclude, the name Mason is clearly an occupational name and its prolific survival may reflect the importance of the mason in medieval society. The surname has many variants, some of which have survived to the present day, the most popular after Mason being Machen, Machin and Machon, which reflect the Norman form of the word.

Sources Consulted

P H Reaney, *The Origins of English Surnames* (London: Routledge & Kegan Paul 1967)

P H Reaney & R M Wilson, *A Dictionary of British Surnames* (London: Oxford University Press, 3rd edition 1995)

P H Reaney, *A Dictionary of British Surnames* (London: Routledge & Kegan Paul, 2nd edition 1976)

P Hanks & F Hodges, *A Dictionary of Surnames* (Oxford University Press 1988)

M A Lower, *Patronymica Brittanica* (London 1860)

C W Bardsley, *A Dictionary of English and Welsh Surnames* (1901: reprinted, Baltimore: Genealogical Publishing Co. 1967)

C L'Estrange Ewen, *Guide to the Origin of British Surnames* (London: John Gifford 1938)

H B Guppy, *Homes of Family Names in Great Britain* (London 1890)

Ernest Weekley, *The Romance of Names* (London: John Murray, 2nd edition 1917)

Ernest Weekley, *Surnames* (London: John Murray 1917)

George F Black, *The Surnames of Scotland* (New York Public Library 1946)

Edward McLysaght, *The Surnames of Ireland* (Dublin: Irish University Press 1977)

T J & Prys Morgan, *Welsh Surnames* (Cardiff: University of Wales Press 1985)

F K & S Hitching, *References to English Surnames in 1601* (Walton on Thames: Bernau 1910)

F K & S Hitching, *References to English Surnames in 1602* (Walton on Thames: Bernau 1911)

The Dictionary of National Biography: Index & Epitome (London 1906)

The Concise Dictionary of National Biography, Part II, 1901-1950, (Oxford 1961)

Burke's Family Index (London: Burke's Peerage Limited 1976)

H R Moulton, Palaeography, Genealogy & Topography (1930)

Prerogative Court of Canterbury Wills (online index)

G W Marshall, *The Genealogist's Guide* (1903)

J B Whitmore, *A Genealogical Guide* (London 1953)

Charles Bridger, *An Index to Pedigrees* (London 1867)

Geoffrey B Barrow, *The Genealogist's Guide* (London: Research Publishing Co. 1977)

Sir Bernard Burke, *The General Armory* (London 1884)

C R Humphrey-Smith, ed, *Burke's General Armory Volume II,* (Tabard Press 1973)

The Return of Owners of Land (1873)

Eilert Ekwall, *The Oxford Dictionary of English Place Names* (4th edition: Oxford 1960)

W J Hardy & W Page, *A Calendar to the Feet of Fines for London and Middlesex*, Vol 1, Richard I - Richard III (1189-1485) (London 1892)

Richard McKinley, *The Surnames of Oxford* (Leopards Head Press 1977)

Richard McKinley, *The Surnames of Sussex* (Leopards Head Press 1988)

Richard McKinley, *The Surnames of Lancashire* (Leopards Head Press 1981)

Richard McKinley, *The Surnames of Norfolk and Suffolk* (Phillimore 1975)

George Redmonds, *The Surnames of Yorkshire West Riding* (Phillimore 1973)

Mr Avenell, *The Norman People* (London 1874)

Debrett's Heraldry (London 1933)

Boutell's Heraldry (Warne 1970)

Online indexes to 1841-1911 Census Returns of England, Wales and Scotland (*Findmypast.com*)

Dictionnaire de Noms et Prénoms de France (Larousse 1951)

The Oxford English Dictionary (Oxford University Press, 2013, online)

J J Kneen, *The Personal Names of the Isle of Man* (Oxford 1937)